A Strangely Wrapped Gift

Emily Juniper

central
avenue
publishing

2020

For everyone who made me who I am,
but especially for:

Valerie, Warren, Sarah, Mary, and John Reardon

Published by Central Avenue Publishing, an imprint of Central Avenue Marketing Ltd.
www.centralavenuepublishing.com

A STRANGELY WRAPPED GIFT

Trade Paperback: 978-1-77168-189-6
Epub: 978-1-77168-190-2
Mobi: 978-1-77168-191-9

Published in Canada
Printed in United States of America

1. POETRY / General   2. POETRY / Women Authors

10 9 8 7 6 5 4 3

Summer – 1

Autumn – 31

Winter – 73

Spring – 113

Leap Year – 163

I was once told that my OCD was a strangely wrapped gift, and though I do not believe mental illness should ever be romanticized, in some ways, I can agree. Not because it made me stronger or better, because I believe I could have become strong in more graceful ways than suffering through mental illness, and not because it is some kind of "beautiful struggle" (it isn't), but because as a teacher and a writer, I have a small platform that I can use to help others that struggle with the same things I have been through. I consider it a gift to be able to look at someone who is where I have been and tell them, with confidence, that it will get better. I consider it a gift to be able to write about mental illness in such a way that helps to end the many dangerous stigmas surrounding the topic (See: people who say "I'm soo OCD," or the idea that suicide is selfish). I consider it a gift to be able to look someone in the eye and tell them they are not crazy, no matter how scary their thoughts might be. Sometimes gifts look questionable until unwrapped. Sometimes bad things happen and good things spring from them. Sometimes gifts are as strange as they are beautiful.

I hope that this book might, in some way, be a strangely wrapped gift for you.

Summer

I ran through

fields of gold

with tan legs and

blueberry-stained lips

and pretended to

be an airplane.

Run, run, run

down the hill.

I would take off toward home,

for where else

would I want to be

in Summer?

(SUMMER)

I grew with roots

planted firmly

inside my mother

and when those roots were ripped, and I was pushed into this world (unwillingly),

I screamed and cried.

And every move since then,

every change,

every uprooting,

I've behaved the same.

(AN AVERSION TO CHANGE)

I was never a princess.

I was always a dragon,
or a jungle queen,
or sometimes a wolf.

I never played with dolls.
I played with bugs,
and my food,
and imaginary dogs.

I never liked dresses.
I liked running around
pants-less or naked
(if I could get away with it).

I was never a princess.

(ALWAYS A DRAGON)

I don't believe in love at first sight,

but I believe in not knowing what you want until you see
it and people too beautiful to absorb and the possibility
of forever.

(THE POSSIBILITY OF FOREVER)

It's one a.m.

Crisp breath,

laced fingers;

the witching hour

belongs to us alone.

The stars,

like sutures,

hold the heavens together

and I think that

we could be eternal.

(1 A.M.)

Unconditional love is not romantic; it's dangerous.

Love should always have conditions.

(CONDITIONS)

1. The hum of the dishwasher in my little home.

2. The rain, the river, the waves and salty wind.

3. My mother's voice, anywhere and always. Moon shadow, moon shadow.

4. The squeaking of an old swing in a schoolyard playground and the laughter of my little brother squealing "higher, Emmy, higher!"

5. Open windows on a hot summer's eve: the crickets, the bullfrogs, and the life-giving sounds of the visceral night.

(SOUNDS THAT COMFORT ME)

She plants

her feet

and

mountains

rise

for her.

(MOUNTAINS)

My bed.

A long run.

The creek behind my childhood home.

A day without the internet.

A swimsuit catalogue with bodies that look like mine.

A book, an hour, and a cup of tea.

You.

(SAFE SPACES)

I trace the stretch marks

on the soft parts of me,

like fissures in the ground

dug by plate tectonics

when the Earth was new,

or mighty canyons

carved by glaciers

during the last ice age.

All things that shaped the world right here,

on the quiet parts

of my body.

(FISSURES)

I remember waking up on Saturdays to the crackling of
fried dough and laughter, and coming down the stairs on
Christmas morning feeling loved beyond imagination,
and I remember lying sunburnt in a field in front of
the house you built thinking, good God, this place is
incredible.

(AN OPEN LETTER TO MY PARENTS)

Here's to the kids

getting high off music

and drunk off books.

Sometimes,

these good drugs

are the only things

keeping them alive.

(GOOD DRUGS)

He wanted a taste of my sweet core

without putting in any work.

But you know what they say:

no worker bees, no fruit.

(DRONE)

Listen, can you hear?

Your pain is telling you something.
Let go of what is hurting you.

(LISTEN)

I'm twenty-something,

but I listen to Jimmy Eat World on my closet floor like I'm fifteen,

and miss my parents like I'm twelve,

and believe in magic and

chocolate for breakfast like I'm eight.

(JIMMY EAT WORLD)

Like a mountain

I rise

in spite of all the men

who think

they have conquered me.

(RISING)

Do not draft

your head into a war

your heart does not believe in.

(HEADS AND HEARTS)

I don't want someone

to put me back together;

I want someone to

love my pieces,

even the jagged ones.

(PIECES)

Do not frown

at the softness of your thighs; do not hide your
tenderness. All the best things are soft:

a mother's womb,

a baby's tummy,

a man's forgiveness,

that space in someone's bed that is only for you.

Don't ever let the world

make you believe

it's not okay to be soft.

(SOFT)

And there she was,

like the night sky,

just inviting me

to be inspired.

(SHE)

It is an insult

to the world

to water yourself

down,

to shallow

your waters,

to dull your shine.

(INSULT)

I am still learning how to love my body

(slowly, softly, gently)

and I am still learning how to be okay on the days when I do not.

(RECOVERY IS NOT LINEAR)

I don't need blood

from anyone

who has wronged me;

revenge is not a

healing language.

(HAMMURABI WAS WRONG)

I want to turn off the news

       but I might miss Trump's next move.

I want to put down my phone

      but if I do, I'll get behind in the groupchat.

I want to delete Facebook

       but I'm afraid I'll be left out.

I want to exit Netflix

      but if I don't keep going, I might see a spoiler.

So I keep the news on

      but get too stressed to leave the house,

and stay on my phone

      but forget the friends in my presence,

and keep scrolling

but miss the sunrise and my own quiet morning thoughts,

and keep watching

      but no longer hear the sound of the rain at night.

Oh, the paradox:

       I am so afraid of missing out

that I miss all the things that happen

       right in front of me.

(PARADOX)

       EMILY JUNIPER

I am never lonelier

than when I am with

the wrong people.

(WRONG PEOPLE)

I look at my sisters,

so kind and smart

and fierce as lightning,

so perfectly imperfect,

and sometimes I cannot believe

they allow men the

privilege of loving them.

(SISTERS)

Someday I'll have a daughter, and I hope the earth trembles a little beneath her feet,

and that Cassiopeia watches over her as she sleeps, and that the greatest love

she ever knows

is in herself.

(CASSIOPEIA)

Autumn

Autumn is seductive.
She calls to me
from a warm hearth,
inviting me with
oversized sweaters
and dates that last
deep into the night.
She breathes a
strange hope of new
beginning into my lungs,
even though I know that
Winter is coming.

(AUTUMN)

Twenty-three.

Three broken teeth

and blood on the hardwood floor.

I fell out of bed

thrashing

from bad dreams,

sweating

from too many covers

-no-

from the crippling weight

of student debt,

self-doubt

and artificial serotonin.

Too heavy, piled high, crushing.

"We're sorry; you seem like a great candidate,

but you have no experience."

But how can I get experience

if no one will hire me?

Oh.

Maybe because I'm lazy,

or busy ruining the economy

by not buying bar soap or property.

"Get a job!"

. . . I already have two,

but I can't even afford the health insurance

I'd need

to fix three broken teeth.

(MILLENNIAL)

Sometimes,

I feel the swell

of the sea in my bones.

Sometimes,

I feel the riptide

of the world

pulling me in

all different directions.

But always,

I feel the ocean

that is you

within me.

(THE OCEAN THAT IS YOU)

I was ten the first time my brain scrambled up like an egg. What if you . . . ? It asked me. (I still can't type it out.) And I threw down the iron shovel because it was such an awful thought. Why would I ever hurt someone I loved? A child should be able to dig tunnels in the snow without dealing with that. It's not right. I didn't ask for it. It didn't even belong to me. The imp of the mind, they call it. A monster. A bad thought knocking down my moral doors like the uninvited drunk aunt at Thanksgiving who just won't leave. For a decade the thought wouldn't leave, so I made rules for myself. No shovels, no knives. In 2009, no forks. Not even pens or pencils. Then, no looking at sharp shapes. No triangles. Nothing pointy. I was in servitude to a master I never asked for, and he never ever let me rest. Like I said, I was ten the first time my brain scrambled up like an egg. I didn't have the words to describe it, but I knew something was wrong.

Very wrong.

(OCD I)

There are no moths
or flames,
just people who know
a bad thing
when they see it,
and go for it anyway.

(MOTH AND FLAME)

A soft rain,

the crickets talking beneath a harvest moon,

and your voice,

breaking the silence like a warm wave.

It all sounds like poetry to me.

(POETRY)

I can be a mermaid,

or I can be a siren;

you decide.

(SIREN)

Put a needle in my hip.

Punch it right into the marrow

(I'll scream).

See?

I told you—

you're in my bones.

(BIOPSY)

And I remember

the worst part of every day

was sunset,

when I knew that soon

everyone would be asleep,

and I would have

nobody

to distract me

from you.

(OCD II)

I still climb trees,

but no longer pretend

I've conquered the world.

I still eat cookie dough,

but worry about raw eggs

and calories.

I still run through the rain,

but jump over the puddles

instead of through them.

I still feel magic

from time to time,

but I think the old ways

might have been easier.

(OLD MAGIC)

Love me like we've

never met.

Like I'm a fantasy

or a wish fulfilled.

Love me like there

might be no tomorrow,

at least not for us.

Love me like

a storm is coming

and you'll be stuck inside

for seven days

with nothing to do

but love me

like you've never

loved me.

(SEVEN DAYS)

Do you ever get that feeling,

that someone will

absolutely,

irreversibly ruin you,

but go for it anyway?

Yeah. Me too.

(RUIN YOU)

I want so badly
to turn you into art,
but I'm afraid.

Afraid that if I carve
you into clay,
I'll jinx something.

Afraid that if you leave,
I'll be stuck with a painting
that only hurts to look at.

But mostly,
I'm afraid no medium
could do you justice.

(TURN YOU INTO ART)

Maybe the castles you build keep crumbling down
because you're looking for a prince(ss)
when you should be looking for yourself.

(FIND YOU)

I dump sugar

carelessly

into my morning coffee

and I wonder

if we too

will dissolve

as soon as we are

done falling.

(COMMUTER THOUGHTS)

I couldn't even find peace in church, because no matter how loudly I prayed, the thoughts screamed louder:

I am bad. I am sick. I am crazy.

God could hear my thoughts,

they said.

Catholic guilt.

I loved my family. They loved me.

Would they if they knew?

Mental illness was not a term

I learned until much later.

(OCD III)

I feel too much

or not enough,

and get upset over things

that exist only in my head.

I am hard to love,

but that doesn't

make me less worthy.

(COULD YOU LOVE SOMEONE LIKE ME?)

The sandpiper

does not dictate

when the waves roll and recede. She must pick for shells
when opportunity strikes, and she must survive

even when the

seas are stormy.

(I AM THE SANDPIPER)

Dear Women,
you are never
being unfair
by saying no.
You are never
being selfish
by asking for
what you want.

(DEAR WOMEN)

I am not a cat,

and if you call

out to me like one,

you will see I am a lion,

and I will bite.

(I AM A LION)

I will not

water down

my words

simply because

you find my tongue

too potent.

(POTENT)

They say we
all have our vices,
so I guess it is fitting
that I have you.

(VICES)

There are wonders of the world

less enticing than the untouched places of you.

(WONDERS OF THE WORLD)

Being with you

made me feel

like every day was

Sunday;

I always knew we had

an expiration date,

and like Monday morning,

it would come too soon.

(LIKE SUNDAY)

I once read

that feeling lonely

means I need to

get to know myself.

But what if I'm lonely

because I know myself too well?

(L O N E L Y)

I went looking for a love that was only for me, not
realizing if I tried to possess love,

it would possess me.

(POSSESSION)

"Table for two, please."

The host points to the back of the gastropub to a dimly lit high top.

"Perfect," we say in unison, my husband and I.

"Can I start you off with a drink?" asks the waiter, a store-bought smile pasted to her face.

"I'll have whatever's on tap."

"Water for me," I say, my hand protectively on a belly that still does not show.

She nods and asks if we'd like to hear the specials, which we've already seen are tuna tartare and veal, but we nod to be polite.

"Tonight our chef has prepared for you your very own eight-ounce contribution to fishless oceans by 2048, and our house favorite: a medallion of calf ripped from his mother at birth and confined to a three-foot-long wooden crate for ninety days before being sent to market. It is an absolute *delicacy*."

My husband gets up to leave, spewing in anger,
  Well, I never!

and I echo him
because going along with the crowd
is always easier than being forced to think about something
we didn't want to know in the first place.

(BLISS)

I'm sure

I left a bitter taste

in your mouth;

I never said

I'd be easy to swallow.

But things that are

good for us

rarely are.

(GOOD FOR YOU)

I want to stay

in this space

with you where

tomorrow doesn't matter,

and yesterday is but a

fading memory.

You and I,

this moment.

That is my forever.

(MY FOREVER)

I never understood the logic behind if they love you, they'll come back, because if they loved you, why would they leave

in the first place?

(PEOPLE ALWAYS LEAVE)

If they cannot give their time,

you cannot* give your love.

(SHOULD NOT*)

I wish

I could be okay

with unrequited love,

but I am not

a wolf,

and you are not the moon.

(WOLF AND MOON)

My skin is dry and creped;

I am dehydrated,

parched,

and only you can

quench my thirst.

(PARCHED)

If God is love,

the devil is infatuation.

I have been tricked

by him more times

than I care to admit.

Lust is a poser.

(INFATUATION)

I give

too many chances

to people who

don't deserve them,

but who could

condemn a heart

that keeps believing

even when it shouldn't?

(CHANCES)

The truth is,

I simply cannot share you,

and if that notion

frightens you,

then I am not

your woman.

(BAD AT SHARING)

You said

maybe a few years from now, as if I were the type of girl
who would gamble

a thousand tomorrows

on the maybe

of a man who couldn't

commit to one of them.

(NOT A GAMBLER)

Don't let anyone

treat you like

a secret

when you know

damn well

you're a revelation.

(REVELATION)

Winter

Warm blood

in cold sheets;

I became a woman

in the Winter.

We all did, I think.

We were born into a cold

that burned,

forced to find warmth

within our sisters, our mothers, ourselves.

I am not afraid of Winter.

(WINTER)

I water your memory with moscato

and fertilize it with

texts from the old days,

until it grows like poison oak,

wrapping around my brain,

forcing me to think of your face,

your voice,

the girl,

the one with the green eyes, the one you loved more.

Maybe if I had any sense

of self-preservation I'd

pour this wine down the drain

and delete the messages,

but I don't care about that.

All I care about is reliving a time when I was happy,

when you were here,

before.

Before this.

Before now.

Before I was sobbing and drunk and so very alone.

(HOW IT IS FOR A WHILE IF THEY LEFT YOU
FOR SOMEONE ELSE)

EMILY JUNIPER

You make

songs

and smells

and places

I used to love,

hurt.

(HURT)

I wish sometimes

I hadn't wasted

my birthday wishes

on silly things like

roller skates and vacations.

Maybe then,

I'd have enough magic left to wish for you.

(BIRTHDAY WISHES)

Love is loud;

heartbreak is louder.

This only seems

pessimistic because

we don't want to believe it.

(THE TRUTH)

Just this once,

let's pretend we can

make love without

summoning the ghosts

of the ones we left behind.

(JUST TONIGHT)

My sister and I
used to drink river water from cupped hands
and collect milkweed
pretending it was *Indian Corn*.

We had watched the movie about the brown-skinned
woman
with almond eyes and a jade necklace
who fell in love with the man from England
—*John Smith*—
who saved her from marrying her betrothed,
who she never really loved.

Little did we know
Pocahontas
was as young as we were,
and playing *native american*
should've been much more traumatic
than drinking river water through cupped hands.

(Disney didn't tell us about the smallpox or the rape or
the forgotten genocide.)
And it was all because of people who looked a lot like us.

(MY FAULT)

Shakespeare taught me things like "Parting is such sweet sorrow."

Call me a cynic,

but I see nothing sweet

about being left alone

after the promise of a lifetime.

(SHAKESPEARE TAUGHT ME)

Not the gallows,

not the guillotine,

not even the water board;

no torture is

worse than

being in love

with a memory, a ghost, just the spirit of a thing I used to
be able to touch.

(THE GALLOWS)

The road wasn't paved with good intentions, it was stricken with them.

Splayed out in the gutters

like casualties or roadkill,

they were devoured

by stronger things like

greed and hunger and whatever was easier.

We called them good intentions because maybe they looked like that at one point

from the outside

but deep down,

we always knew why

we did what we did.

(HOW WE GOT TO HELL)

The anxiety you feel

is just a scared little child.

Hold her,

dry her tears,

and promise her

you've got this.

Because you do.

(ON ANXIETY)

These three little letters

hang around my neck

like a dead albatross,

bad luck always

(or something like it).

They haunt me

like a spectre

and nag me

like an endless list

of to-dos that serve

no purpose at all.

(OCD IV)

1850.

They said "get rich quick"

so we hopped a train to San Francisco, pyrite, and lies.

2012.

Here we lie,

sifting through one another

like hands through cold river water

looking for something shiny

but finding only dust,

empty promises,

and fool's gold.

(FOOL'S GOLD)

We must feel the tears of the river,

the crying of the dwindling forest

and the bellowing of the windowless slaughterhouse

the same way we feel the hearts beating in our chests.

We must recognize that their suffering is our suffering.

Only then can we save ourselves.

(WE ARE ALL CONNECTED)

I am a donut. Cinnamon sugar, Boston cream. You think I'm kidding, but look at me. Soft, sweet, and easy to chew. Nobody chokes on me, but nobody wants me at every meal. Sure, I'm more appealing than a salad, but nobody makes me a lifestyle. Do you know how exhausting it is, being sweet all the time and then being called too easy? Do you know how hard it is knowing I'll always be stale by morning?

(DONUT)

He stuck me in a blue pot,

covered me with soil

and commanded love to grow.

Silly boy,

you cannot quicken nature

and you cannot rush my love,

even if your hands are good

at getting dirty.

(BLUE POT)

Dark Blue

like my favorite song

or a thunderstorm in mid-July.

Like dead rose petals and

fallen stars and your

breath on a cold winter night.

Like the single shadow

that follows me around,

a constant reminder

that there used to be two.

(DARK BLUE)

You're so unorganized,

they said,

you can't have OCD.

I wish I hadn't learned about OCD from people who didn't know anything about OCD.

Maybe then,

I'd have gotten help sooner.

Maybe then,

I wouldn't have spent

my whole life

thinking I was crazy.

Maybe then,

I could've gotten help

the first time

my brain whispered

". . ."

I won't tell you what my brain whispered; I'm not ready yet.

(O C D V)

EMILY JUNIPER

It is not romantic;

it's painful

and consuming

and the memory of it

never,

ever

fades.

(FORBIDDEN LOVE)

You didn't have to break me just to prove that you are
whole.

(BREAK)

I look at her

and through the looking glass I go,

tumbling, falling, grasping, clawing,

trying to hold on to a reality

that was never mine to begin with.

In the mirror, they're my own eyes

but I no longer know

the mind that lives behind them.

(DEPERSONALIZATION)

I pulled out a sore tooth one night with pliers and closed eyes. A twelve-year molar, I think. Oh, it bled and I screamed, but later I felt better.

The tooth was rotten.

The tooth was you.

(ROT)

Go ahead and be
angry with me,
as if shouting at a tornado
will undo the catastrophe.
As if punching back
will resolve the fight.
Go ahead and yell,
but remember that
it will only deepen
your own wounds.

(GO AHEAD)

I try to tell myself

that you are just a

blip on a rock in an

insignificant universe,

and that someday you will

burn out like our sun

and everything else.

That you are nothing but

flesh and bone,

and in time you will be only bone, and in even more time
you will be dust.

I try to tell myself this,

but I have never been a

good liar.

(BAD LIAR)

You have tick-bite love,

my dear.

Spreading slowly,

causing sickness and lethargy for years to come because
of one godforsaken night together.

(TICK BITE)

We're out of sync.

Call it a rut or

blame Mercury in retrograde—

whatever makes you feel better

about the tessellations we have become.

Whatever makes you forget about the topaz mosaic we
thought we'd be.

(TESSELLATE)

How do you combat a foe who lives inside your mind?

You love yourself.

And forgive yourself.

And let yourself be helped. And work and work and work

until the demons dance a little quieter.

And then you do it again.

(ON MENTAL ILLNESS)

It is by fate we met

and by fate we part,

but it is by my will alone

that we stay apart.

Because fate

is never an excuse

for abuse.

(FATE)

I always find you

at the bottom of my wine glass. I don't even have to be drunk; I find you at the bottom of everything.

(AT THE BOTTOM OF IT)

"They are just scars;

they don't hurt."

"I am not afraid."

"I don't love you anymore."

Who says make believe

is only for children?

I do it all the time.

(MAKE BELIEVE)

So you're telling me

they can put

screws through my bones

and staples in my skin,

but there still isn't anything

to soothe a broken heart

except whiskey and wine?

(WHISKEY AND WINE)

I walk around

with half a heart

on my sleeve

and the other half

locked in a steel cage,

the key to which

I gave away ages ago.

(HEART STUFF)

Cry for Syria.

Cry for FGM in Somalia

that will never make the news.

Cry for veal calves and bullfights and elephants and bees.

Cry for girls who think

their worth is measured by the size of the gap between their thighs.

I could go on and on,

but I've run out of

paper and tears.

(PAPER AND TEARS)

I am not a ship to sail

or a wave to ride,

no,

I am a fucking ocean

to get lost in,

a sea full of sirens

that can either

return your love

or swallow you whole.

(A SEA FULL OF SIRENS)

EMILY JUNIPER

The wreckage

will never be as bad

as the storm.

If you are looking at the wreckage, the hardest part is
over.

Now you need only to

recover.

(THE WRECKAGE)

You were

the best thing

and the worst thing,

euphoria

and tragedy

wrapped in a tight

little package.

It was exciting

and heartbreaking

and real,

but it wasn't

meant to last.

And I have

made peace

with that.

(ACCEPTANCE)

I cannot recall

the last time

I woke up and felt okay,

but that doesn't mean

I won't feel okay again.

(HOPE)

Spring

She's subtle.

She doesn't bloom

overnight;

she knows

that good things

take time.

(SPRING)

I know you think you're damaged goods, but we all are.

We carry around pieces

of old lovers,

and people who've died,

and dogs who ran away when we were young.

We've got scars and bruises

and wisdom that was ripped from our mouths because a dentist said it would ruin the orthodonture.

We've got old love letters stashed away in boxes, and pictures of friends we used to know

and text messages we can't delete even though it's been two years.

But isn't it beautiful that someone out there

will see your brokenness and be perfectly okay with it, because they understand it too.

(UNDAMAGED GOODS)

There is strength in forgiveness but there is wisdom in knowing when to walk away.

(WISDOM)

(S)he is not the ocean;
You are the ocean.
(S)he is nothing
but a ship that
crashed upon
your shore.

((S)HE IS NOT THE OCEAN)

Do you think we are
destined for greatness?

I think we are
destined for something.

So she hollowed you out

like a pumpkin,

scraped out all of your innards and replaced them with
dead air.

But do you know what?

She left all of this space in you

to be filled with good things, happy things,

things that deserve to be

inside of you.

(HOLLOW)

You can only love me

if you can accept that

I will sometimes be

hard to love.

(HOW TO LOVE ME)

You are filled with hurt,

but you are also filled with potential.

(POTENTIAL ENERGY)

No one will save you
from the monsters
in your head but yourself,
and you are going to
have to work for it.

(ON RECOVERY)

Take a break from it—
all of it.
Step back and observe the
beauty of your fight.
You can continue tomorrow but for now,
just. breathe.

(BREATHE)

I'm stuck in the muck of unloving you,

this purgatory between love and hate.

The first, I once did;

the latter, I never could.

But I can hate myself for not loving you

(as well I should),

while I sit and wait for God and the devil to decide what they're going to do with me.

(PURGATORY)

I stayed because I loved you
and then I left
because I loved myself.

(STAYING AND LEAVING)

EMILY JUNIPER

Tonight is the new moon

(the sky is dark)—

she and I

are mourning

your loss together.

But we will soon

be bright and full again,

hardly able to remember

the pains of the past.

(THE MOON AND I)

It is a strangely wrapped gift.

The wrong person
saying goodbye

at the right time.

(A STRANGELY WRAPPED GIFT)

Stay alive for me.

For me,

just a girl

you don't know

typing in a coffee shop

in somewhere, USA.

Promise me;

promise me you

will stay alive

for me.

I want to live

in a world

that has you in it.

(ON SUICIDE)

I once knew a man

who treated me

like a punching bag,

and I once knew a man

who treated me

like a shield,

and I knew a few who

treated me

like a glass doll.

But my favorite man

was the one who treated me like a garden.

Who planted himself next to me, and watered me,

and sheltered me from the weeds, and pushed me toward
the sun.

(MEN I'VE KNOWN)

The flowers never tell the sun how much they love her, but if she burned out, the whole earth would scream.

That is how I feel for you. If you left, my world would bend in half and never straighten out, and I wrote these words because I want you to know that I am the flowers and you are the sun. And I need you to know that you are not just rising and setting to kill time. You are not just living to get to the next sleep. You are lighting up so many skies and you don't even know it, you radiant, electric star. I am not asking you to stay for me; I'm begging you to stay for you. And for the flowers. And for tomorrow. And for all of the tomorrows after that.

(SUNBURST)

I was a gluttonous child,

an envious, insecure teenager,

and my lust for things

floated me through my early twenties.

But I am a good, honest person

and if I can be good

after these deadly sins,

so then can you.

(THREE SINS)

Taking a serotonin pill

does not make you weak.

Neither does refusing it.

(ZOLOFT)

It's okay

if sunlight strangles you,

if the air always feels too heavy,

and if walking out the front door

is scarier than a thousand hissing snakes.

(ON DEPRESSION)

It is true that while

you are falling in love,

someone else

is being broken,

and while you are

birthing your first child,

someone else

is losing theirs,

and while you lie in bed,

alone and confused,

someone else is

finally figuring it out.

I can't decide

whether this is

beautiful or tragic,

but I think

it might be

both.

(BEAUTIFUL AND TRAGIC)

And there will come a day
when you come alone,
but do not leave that way.

(COMING AND GOING)

I am not the sunflower, thrusting boldly toward the sky.

I am the seedling

pushing through the cracks

in the tennis court.

And the wildflower growing in the garden, accidentally
planted by the wind.

And the water lily,

too short to break the surface,

always fighting for the sun.

Growing is not easy for me;

I have never been a natural,

but like nature,

I always find a way.

(GROWING)

Do not weep
for lost love.
Weep only
for lost time.

(WEEP)

Accept

that the old him

may not be the new him,

or that maybe the old you

is not the new you

and you have outgrown him.

(OUTGROWN)

Your vibrance does not diminish when someone fails to see it. Can't you see?

The wolf does not stop howling

just because the moon does not answer.

(WOLF AND MOON II)

They did not make you stronger.

They did not make you better.

They simply complemented a time in your life.

But that time has passed,

and you are not broken because you have lost, and you are not damaged because you are hurting.

(YOU DO NOT NEED THEM)

Wait for the one

who can prove to you

that it doesn't always have to hurt.

Then make them prove it.

(PROOF)

I don't want you to just

admire my outsides

and tell me I'm pretty.

I want you

to want to unfold me

like an origami crane

and see where I came from.

I want you to feel the scars

on my paper wings

and know that the girl

standing before you had trouble learning how to fly.

(PAPER CRANE)

I'm a gift on Christmas morning,

and you're a heavy thumb and rough forefinger

tearing away at my wrapping-paper skin,

trying to get to what is underneath.

I wonder,

will you cherish it forever,

hand it down,

or pretend to love it but return it the morning after?

(PLAYTHING)

They will try to make their ignorance louder than your love.

They will try to make their fear louder than your cries for justice.

They will try to make their comfort zone louder than your safety.

They try to make it about the constitution or bathrooms or God,

but there is nothing godly about hate.

(GOD AND HATE)

I think about all the times you took care of me. And the
times I shed tears into your collar bones when I was
too ashamed to look you in the eye. About the way you
rubbed my back until I felt better, was better. I think
about the times you made me laugh when I didn't think
I had it in me, and the times I cried from the immensity
of your love. I think about how the sunrise is the color of
your smile, and how the twilight is the same weight as
your love. A thick wool blanket keeping me warm. Snug
and tight. Safe. A reprieve from the chaos of the day. I
think about all of these things when I think of you, and
you, and you and you and you. And how lucky I am to
have written this, and to not be sure whom it's about,
because I have known so much love. Yours. And yours.
And yours and yours and yours. And how I hope I am
the color of the sunrise and the warm cover of twilight for
someone else. Someday, at least.

(L U C K Y)

I'm not going to
pretend that
what you did to me
was okay
just because
I learned something.

(NOT OKAY)

Five things to know:

You have been loved.

You are loved.

You will be loved again.

You will get through it, no matter what it is.

You are not alone,

even when you feel the heavy weight of loneliness.

(FIVE THINGS)

I cannot imagine this world without you; that is how fiercely you belong.

(THERE IS ALWAYS ONE PERSON WHO FEELS THIS WAY ABOUT YOU)

I walked into your garden

looking for something:

growth,

or maybe clarity,

but all I found was parched earth in need of a gardener.

And I'm sorry,

but for once,

I cannot be the fixer

in the relationship.

(FIXER)

I have a rabbit heart

and salty tears

(so many of them)

and the downy wings

of a gosling that can't yet fly.

But I am getting there,

oh, I am getting there.

(GETTING THERE)

I am just a traveler

on a worn-out road

picking up snippets

of others' conversations,

listening for someone

I've never met.

I leave footprints

like scars on the sandy path,

a path that's been scarred before.

You've been here, haven't you? Trying to get over
something, or someone.

Trying to leave it all behind.

Yes,

this road is a crowded one.

(TRAVELER)

Some nights you unzip me like a dress,

careful not to snag my lace or scratch my delicate skin.

I raise my arms and you slip your hands

under the heavy fabric of the day,

and I can tell you feel the bumps and bruises it left on me

but you don't blink an eye,

you just slide the pretty facade over my head

until all the weight is gone and I can fall into you

exactly as I am.

(NAKED)

I often ask the stars

what they would do

if they were me,

but they just keep shining.

So I do too.

(ASKING THE STARS)

I built a home in ~~you~~ me

and when you left

I ~~was left~~ still possessed

~~with nothing~~ all I needed.

(REVISION)

I tried to write about you,

but didn't get very far.

It was like trying to

capture a sunset

with a photo,

or describe my favorite song

using only sign language.

No words,

however beautiful,

could do you justice.

(UNWRITTEN)

EMILY JUNIPER

I spent my whole life

fighting currents,

but now

I think I'll stay

and tread water

with you for a while.

Or forever.

(TREADING WATER)

Everything about you
makes me wonder
if I have ever really loved,
or been loved
before.

(YOU)

I hope my daughters are born

with the strength that I have worked for.

(DAUGHTERS)

The night may be dark,

but we, my love,

are lucent.

(LUCENT)

The universe does not revolve around you; the universe is within you.

(FOR YOU ARE THE UNIVERSE)

I've told you

you are the ocean,

you are the universe,

yet still you are more.

You are the sun, the rain,

and life and death.

You don't believe me?

But how many times have

you felt like nothing?

So many times,

so many times.

Just this once,

give yourself a chance

to believe that you

are everything.

(BECAUSE YOU ARE)

Leap Year

1995. My favorite teddy ripped down the seams and my mother said it was well loved. Twelve years later a boy split me in two, but I knew better. I wasn't torn apart by the immensity of love. I was simply an expendable toy he could not be bothered to mend.

(TEDDY)

You slip into my worn-out sneakers
but blisters do not form
on your heels,
'cause walking in another's shoes
is never as simple as saying
you would have done things differently.

Well of course you would have.

It's easy to walk in shoes
that are already broken in.

(BLISTERS)

They ask how I spent my whole life not knowing I was
gay.

I tell them *a tiger raised in captivity does not realize
it is trapped.*

(29)

There's a reason mouse poison works—

sometimes, toxic things are hard to resist.

Remember, not everything that goes down like honey is good for you.

(TOXIC)

Our house has an old soul.

There are books with yellowing pages,

cracked windows,

two cups of lukewarm tea.

Heat it up again

till it's just right

and the house is full

of chamomile and dark honey,

and your eyes are full of my body,

and your ears are swollen with my voice

and whispers no one else

has ever heard.

(OLD SOUL)

Fresh

like snowdrops poking out of the ground in mid-March

or soft baby skin.

She wears dried lavender in her hair

and burns sage in the living room

to ward off the bad thoughts

that pay her visits

in the night.

She tucks herself in

with iPhone carpal tunnel syndrome

and Lexapro.

Nothing's simple anymore,

but perhaps

it never ever was.

(NEW SOUL)

Dandelion,
I ask,
are you a flower, or a weed?

It depends,
she says,
on where I choose to grow.
In another's garden
fighting for attention betwixt the tulips
I am but a lowly weed,
but in an open field
where little girls go to pick wildflowers
and blow me with wishes into the wind,
I am most certainly a flower.

The moral?
Grow where you have room to flourish;
don't force yourself into a garden
that's already been sown.

(WHAT THE DANDELION TAUGHT ME)

Sometimes I get out of bed and my heart and head hurt for no reason or for reasons I can do nothing about. Like pigs stuck in farrowing crates, squealing and banging their heads out of boredom, or children stuck in cages at the border crying for their mamas. Sometimes I despair over lost friendships I'll do nothing about because I'd rather sit home on a Friday night than actually talk to another human being. And then I won't talk for years but still want them to love me. Sometimes I'm so happy I'm high but it's like waiting for a guillotine to drop because I know it won't last. I jump out of bed and make a to-do list and sing and dance while I clean the kitchen but two hours later I'm crying because I could only get through one to-do and feel like a failure. I'm like a pogo stick, up and down, up and down, never knowing when I'll fall. Never knowing when I'll rise. I guess I'm hard to love. I don't know.

(RAMBLES)

It was a habit of mine:
making mountains out of men
as if love were something to be conquered
(a picture at the top,
popped foot, hand on hip,
a hundred and twenty-one likes).

I was wrong
to liken love to Everest,
where only a few make it
to the top
—where only a handful
make it at all.

I was wrong
to justify the pain
with a fleeting view from the summit.
For love should be steady like the river
and endless as the sea.

And it shouldn't be this damn hard.

(TO MAKE MOUNTAINS OUT OF MEN)

I often wonder about heaven:

If it exists,

if it's forever,

what forever looks like,

and if I'll still be thinking of you even in the afterlife.

(HEAVEN)

I cannot seem to open my mouth
without little parts of you
slipping out like sneezes
that can't be held in.

I guess the stories
make me feel closer to you,
and I guess that
is all part of the healing.

(THE PROCESS)

One, two, three.

I count my eggs and put them in your basket,

but your hands aren't delicate —

they cannot hold it steady

so they crack

(one, two, three).

Yellow yolk oozes through the woven belly of the basket.

And you want me to give you my heart?

Please.

You can't even keep the groceries safe.

(YOLK)

You don't hum anymore.
I remember you skipping 'round the kitchen
in cotton shorts
making cocoa,
pretending it was coffee,
humming lullabies the moon or your mother taught you,
talking about how you couldn't wait till nine months
passed,
talking about painting the spare room elephant-grey
so he or she could decide for themselves who they
wanted to be,
telling me they would grow up and fix the world;
you could feel it.

You'd put my hand on your belly
and even though it was too early for kicks
it was fun to pretend.
Spring came and Summer
but never the kicks,
and nine months came and went,
and it's just you and me in the kitchen
drinking caffeinated anything
and the elephant-grey room is full of boxes and old
guitars and invisible sadness
—so much sadness—
and you don't hum
                              anymore.

(HUM)

I fold the map in half until our hearts touch, but I can't
feel yours beating anymore beneath the paper veins.
I look at the moon, the same one that shines in your
window, but it's nine a.m. where you are so you're
looking at the sun—the golden hour, the golden hair of
a girl you think you love. I unfold the map and hope the
multiverse is real and that in another life you and I still
exist as one under the same November moon.

(CHEATED)

Snails

crawl out of your mouth.

I wait

for you to tell me you love me.

I watch

and only see you loving her.

I fly away,

for birds like me

do not have time to pick at shells

of indecisive little mollusks

when there are so many fish

in the beautiful sea.

(SNAILS)

I cut off my left hand

(I don't use it much)

and threw it in a pot

with bitter chocolate,

six oysters

and your old flannel shirt.

A pinch of salt,

and cayenne pepper

for heat

(not that we ever needed it).

A fair trade:

a hand for a heart,

but magic takes time,

so I watch it all boil and wait

for our love to be born again.

(ALCHEMY)

And it was there

during that final twilight

before the Earth collided with oblivion

that we learned holiness and religion,

life and death,

love and eternity

have very little to do with one another after all

and that most of it is just a cosmic cocktail

of luck and timing and the need to feel like we belong

to something

—or someone—

bigger than ourselves.

(BLACK HOLE)

1. The coffee shop on 8th and Main where we met for the first time in broad daylight because I was too afraid to meet a perfect stranger after dark.

2. The corner of the living room, where the cobwebs gather because you were the only one who ever cleaned.

3. The drive-in. The Galleria. Under the sycamore tree where we used to read old books.

4. The little stone house we swore we'd buy someday. The one with the broken shutters and the yellow door.

5. The throbbing corner of my brain that cannot seem to shut you off.

(PLACES I FIND YOUR GHOST)

EMILY JUNIPER

Tick tick tick.

(one-two-three)

Drip drip drip

(four-five-six)

Lub-dub, lub-dub, lub-dub

(seven-eight-nine)

The clocks. The leaky sinks. My own heartbeat at night
when there's nothing to drown out the noise.

Madness waxes and wanes as I count

and try not to count

then count some more,

And since I cannot sleep

I lie awake and think of sheep,

And now I'm counting them too;

Into oblivion they go

(one-two-three).

(OCD VI)

On my knees
(not) in church.

On thousand-mile drives
wondering how easy it'd be
to drive off the road
or the edge of existence.

In the eyes of men
I made false idols out of
because I could not find the will
to love myself.

Here,
here,
with you
because sometimes
we don't believe in God
until we've touched something holy with our own two
hands.

(I FOUND GOD WHERE HE WASN'T SUPPOSED
TO BE)

EMILY JUNIPER

See the hand working with no glove.

See the blisters, the boils, the angry red welts.

Then see how the calluses form.

How the skin grows thicker. How it doesn't let the hurt back in.

Hearts can learn a lot from hands,

don't you think?

(HEARTS AND HANDS)

1. My family. My friends. The one who found her way back to me last year by the grace of healed wounds, forgiveness, and love.

2. The hours, the days, the years we spent together. I will never forget. I will never not cherish everything. Everything.

3. My body. So often I hated this holy vehicle that carries my soul, and for that I am sorry, but someone once told me *thank yous* are more meaningful than *I'm sorrys*. So I thank this skin, muscle, and bone. I thank the stretch marks, the tear ducts, the scars.

4. That for the first time in years, food is something I look forward to. That my head is letting food nourish my body, and not forcing me to rob my cells of it as soon as it's consumed. That I do not (and will not) ever have to crouch in secret over a toilet again. That the scabs on my knuckles have healed.

5. That you found me when I was ready to find you. That I opened the window, and it was you who helped me climb out.

(THINGS I'M THANKFUL FOR)

Emily Juniper is the author of three poetry collections (*Things I Learned in the Night, Swim,* and *A Strangely Wrapped Gift*) and a guided journal for mental health and wellness (*One Day at a Time*). She currently resides in upstate New York, is a part of the LGBTQ community, and is an advocate for mental health awareness in kids and teens. In her spare time, she enjoys writing, hiking mountains, iced coffee, validating people's feelings, and working with young writers.

You can find her on Instagram

@evergreen.reveries